Biff's Opposites

Written by Annemarie Young,
based on the original characters
created by Roderick Hunt and Alex Brychta

Illustrated by Alex Brychta

OXFORD
UNIVERSITY PRESS

Biff and Chip both had a cold,
so they were staying indoors.
Kipper was playing with Floppy
in the garden.

"Let's look at our photos,"
said Biff.

"Good idea," said Chip. "Some
of them are really funny."

"We were really **slow** going up
that hill," said Biff.

"But we were very **fast** coming back down," laughed Chip.

"Remember when the hat fell
off the snowman?" asked Biff.

"Yes, it fell **on** Floppy," said
Chip. "He looked very funny."

"Remember when Dad fell **asleep**
after we went sledging?" said Biff.

"But not for long," said Chip.
"He was soon **awake**!"

"It was really **hot** that day, but
it was good fun," said Biff.

"It was too **cold** that day, and
it wasn't fun at all," said Chip.

"Floppy doesn't like being **wet** when he has a bath," said Biff.

"But he really likes being **dry** after the bath," said Chip.

"Dad looked funny with **long** hair," said Biff.

"And Mum looked funny with very **short** hair," laughed Chip.

new

"Remember when Kipper's
teddy was **new**?" asked Biff.

"He's **old** now, but Kipper still loves him," said Chip.

"Floppy looked so **sad** after
he cut himself," said Biff.

"But he was **happy** when we
gave him a new bone," said Chip.

"It was a long way **up** that roller coaster," said Biff.

"And it was really scary going
down," said Chip.

"Floppy made the floor very
dirty that day," said Biff.

"It was hard work mopping
it **clean**," said Chip.

"Oh no! We'd better start mopping
again!" laughed Biff.

Talk about opposites

Pairing opposites

Find the 7 pairs of opposites.

empty

thin

small

loud

high

soft

light

heavy

hard

quiet

thick

full

low

big

Find the opposites

Find as many pairs of opposites as you can in the picture.

(top/bottom; up/down; high/low; open/shut; full/empty; thick/thin; asleep/awake; big/small; short/tall)